NO WORDS
JUST
LOVE

Gianna Becomes a **Big Sister**

Written by **Jerry Alcoser**

Illustrated by **Elena Yalcin**

No Words **Just Love**
Gianna Becomes a **Big Sister**

Written by Jerry Alcoser
Illustrated by Elena Yalcin

Printed in the United States of America
ISBN-13: 979-8-99955-933-3

DEDICATION

To my **husband**, whose love makes our days warm and safe.
To my **Dad, Mom** and **Aunt Ange,** whose care, joy, and steady
support remind us we are never alone.

Together, you make raising a **special needs child** a journey
filled with **courage, kindness**, and **love beyond words.**

Jerry Alcoser

NO WORDS
JUST
LOVE

Gianna Becomes a Big Sister

Written by **Jerry Alcoser**

Illustrated by **Elena Yalcin**

In **NO WORDS JUST LOVE**, Gianna showed us that love **doesn't need words.**

Now, something **new** is happening...

Gianna loved quiet mornings and playing with her sister **Eva.** Eva **always knew how** Gianna liked things— **just so.**

One day, **Eva** leaned in close and whispered,
"We're going to have a baby."

Gianna blinked and looked at Mama's belly.

The **house** started **to change** —
new toys, new sounds.

Gianna **lined up** the number blocks — just the way **she liked**.

Eva helped fold **tiny clothes**.
"They're for **the baby**," she said.

One morning, Mama **wasn't home.**

Nana and **Aunt Ange** came to help — with **cookies** and **hugs.**

"The baby is here!" Daddy said with a smile.
Eva held Gianna's hand as they waited.

Gianna peeked at him and gently touched **his nose**.
Gianluca yawned and made a **squeaky sound**.

Gianna watched quietly, **unsure.**
Eva placed a **soft bear** beside Gianluca.

At nap time, **Gianna** sat near his crib. She **didn't speak** — but she **stayed**.

Eva read a **story** while Gianluca slept.
Gianna turned the pages **with care**.

That night, all **three cuddled** on the couch.
Gianna reached out and **held** her baby brother's **hand.**

"**He's part of our family now,**" Eva said.

Mama exhaled a sigh of **relief** and smiled knowing Gianna **had accepted** her little **brother.**

Gianna **didn't use words** — but she said everything with **love**.

For families with **quiet hearts, big feelings, and growing love** — this story is **for you.**

From the author of

NO WORDS **JUST LOVE**

Resources for Families and Caregivers

Every child's voice matters — whether it's spoken, signed, tapped, or felt through shared moments of connection. These trusted tools and communities can help families support communication, confidence, and belonging.

Speech & Communication Tools

Proloquo2Go
An award-winning augmentative and alternative communication (AAC) app by AssistiveWare. It helps nonverbal or minimally verbal children express themselves using symbols, text, and voices.
👉 www.assistiveware.com/products/proloquo2go

TD Snap 📱
A symbol-based AAC app created by Tobii Dynavox, designed to support communication through visual grids, customizable vocabulary, and voice output. It grows with each child's language skills and is available across multiple devices. There are 7 different versions of TD Snap inside of the software allowing for personalization for each and every child or adult with Autism, no matter the language or speech concern. TobiiDynavox also provides an ecosystem of support and training no matter your location.
👉 www.tobiidynavox.com/tdsnap

Core Boards for Speech 🧩

Visual communication boards featuring essential "core" vocabulary — like want, go, help, more — that children can point to during everyday activities. These tools create structure, confidence, and consistency across home and classroom routines.

👉 Explore Core Boards at Region 4 Education Service Center

ASL (American Sign Language) for Kids 🤟

Introducing simple signs — such as more, help, love, and thank you — gives children early ways to share needs, express affection, and connect with those around them.

💖 Sensory & Emotional Support

Young, Wild & Friedman Sensory Kits 🌿

Hands-on, themed sensory play kits that nurture imagination, calm the senses, and support emotional regulation through creative play.

👉 youngwildandfriedman.com

🌼 A Gentle Reminder

There is no single way to communicate — only many beautiful ways to connect. Through patience, play, and love, families build bridges of understanding that last a lifetime.

ABOUT THE AUTHOR

Jerry Alcoser is an engineer who has worked on projects around the world and a dedicated mother of three, including a special needs child. As a mother of a non verbal autistic child, she understands firsthand the challenges of advocating for the right resources and support to ensure her children thrive.

Her journey has inspired her to create stories that uplift and empower children, reminding them that they are bound for greatness, regardless of the obstacles they face. Through her stories, she also aims to bring awareness to the importance of empathy and kindness in our communities.

A portion of the proceeds from her books will be donated to organizations that support families struggling to help their children thrive, spreading hope and compassion one story at a time.